PULL UP YOUR SOCKS

How to Start a Thriving Freelance Writing Career With Zero Experience

ABDULGANIY SHEHU

Copyright

All rights reserved. No part of this publication **Pull up Your Socks** may be reproduced, stored in a retrieval system or transmitted in any form or by any means, electronic, mechanical, photocopying, recording, scanning or by any inform without permission in writing by the author.

Legal Disclaimer

This book and the content provided therein are simply for educational purposes and to serve as a guide to starting a career in freelance writing. All information in this book are deemed accurate as at the time of publishing. However, this is not an extensive overview of the subjects and expert opinions may differ.

Any use of this information is at your own risk. The author does not assume and hereby disclaims any liability to any party or any loss, damage or disruptions caused by errors or omissions resulting from accident, negligence or any other cause.

No guarantees of income or profits whatsoever are intended by this book. There are a lot of factors that can affect an individual's results.

The results given here might be different from the one you get. The author does not accept responsibility for your results. If you wish to apply ideas contained in this book, you are taking full responsibility for your choices, actions and results.

Printed in the United States of America
© 2018 by AbdulGaniy Shehu

Gilob Publishing House
9577, Creek Rd, Chino Hills
CA 91709
California
USA

Contents

Contents

Reviews by Experts iv

Introduction 1

Why You Should Consider a Career as A Freelance Writer 1

Chapter 1: Sidestep Your Fears: Why You Should Start Writing Today 5

Still Thinking of Writing? Here are 7 Reasons Why You Should: Expresses your personality 7

Gives you Credibility 7

Aids Networking 8

An Essential Job Skill 8

It's a Profession 9

Means of Communication 9

You Can Make a Living Writing 10

Why not Sidestep Your Fears? 10

Chapter 2: Taking Actions: The Newbie Writer's Guide to Success 12

Chapter 3: SO, You Want to Write? 10 Ways to Get Started 20

The Hardest Part is Beginning 21

Follow a Writing Process 21

CHAPTER 4: The Best and Only Way to Learn Writing 27

Eager to Begin a Freelance Writing Career? 5 Things you Must Know 34

What Do You Observe? 36

CHAPTER 6: 10 Successful Tips for Beginner Freelance Writers.......... 45

CHAPTER 7: Top 10 Challenges of A Beginner Freelance Writer (And How to Overcome Them) 54

CHAPTER 8: 7 Daily Productivity Hacks for Freelance Writers 68

CHAPTER 9: 10 Social Media Productivity Hacks for Freelance Writers ... 74

CHAPTER 10: Dealing with Procrastination as a Freelance Writer: A Personal Experience 85

CHAPTER 11: The Defining Moments of a Beginner Freelance Writer 92

About the Author 105

Conclusion 108

Connect with Me 110

Reviews by Experts

What Freelance Writing Experts Say About The Book

"If you're a beginner writer looking to get into freelance writing, give this book a shot! Not only does AbdulGaniy Shehu share practical information to help you overcome your fears, stop being involved in "motion" and actually start taking "action," he also shares relevant **examples and analogies to help drive his points home."**

Bamidele Onibalusi |Founder, Writers In Charge|

"This book by AbdulGaniy Shehu is a must read for any newbie freelance writer who wants to get started with their writing career. It's full of golden nuggets and actionable tips that will take you to greater heights"

Aisha Sulaiman |Freelance Writer| |Blogger|

"This book by AbdulGaniy Shehu is, no doubt, a valuable addition to the subject of freelance writing. It teaches in lucid terms, the right way to start a successful freelance writing career and how you can put your best foot forward. You can never get tired reading this book because of the rare insights and the practical tips it's filled with. I therefore urge you to get yourself a copy and read it"

Hafiz Akinde |Freelance Blogger| |Content Markete

Introduction

Why You Should Consider a Career as A Freelance Writer

The Freelance economy is soaring, and millennials are keying into it. In the United States alone, there are about 53 million people doing freelance work. In the EU labour market, the gig economy (as it's fondly called) is growing faster. Freelancers are the fastest growing group in the EU labour market with their numbers increasing by 45% from just under 6.2 million to 8.9 million in 2013.

The reality is that, freelancing has come to stay. Many have accepted it as a job, and the numbers will continue increasing.

Freelance writing, an integral part of online business accounts for a large chunk of the gig economy.

Freelance writers fill this void by creating content for their clients all over the world. They are involved in series of activities such as web content creation, guest posting, ghost writing, lead generation, feature writing, B2B/B2C writing and the list is endless.

In a bid to make a living through writing. I see many beginners who are eager to join the industry but don't know where or how to start. They don't know what it takes to be successful as a beginner in freelance writing. At the end of the day, they end up dejected, and quit afterwards.

To address this, I've written this book to answer the basic questions of beginner freelance writers. With it, you will understand the freelance writing industry better, and achieve relative success within a short period of time.

The e-book is made up of eleven chapters, and touches all the basic aspects of freelance writing for a beginner. These include:

- Sidestep your fears: Why You Should Start Writing Today?
- Taking Actions: The Newbie Writer's Guide to Success
- So, You Want To Write? 10 Ways To Get Started
- The Best and Only Way To Learn Writing
- Eager to begin a Freelance Writing Career? 5 Things You Must Know
- 10 Successful Tips for Beginner Freelance Writers
- Top 10 Challenges of a Beginner Freelance Writer (And How to overcome them)
- 7 Daily Productivity Hacks for Freelance Writers
- 10 Social Media Productivity Hacks for Freelance Writers
- Dealing with Procrastination as a Freelance Writer: A Personal Experience
- The Defining Moments of a Beginner Freelance Writer

After reading this book, I'm sure your knowledge of freelance writing as a beginner will never remain the same. I hope your target of making it as a beginner freelance writer is met.

Chapter 1

Sidestep Your Fears: Why You Should Start Writing Today

> *"If you don't want to be forgotten as soon as you are dead and rotten in the grave, either write something worth reading or do something worth Writing."*
>
> *- Benjamin Franklin*

Every day, I see wannabe writers, afraid of starting a writing career. Many are afraid because of the notion that writing is hard. Others think that they do not have the requisite skills to command a clout of active followers. Not only that, several others do not know why they should start writing.

I want you to sidestep your fears and do nothing but write. In this chapter, I want to reveal why you should pick up your pen and put down your thoughts, or switch on your computer, and start writing.

But before that; let me tell you this: *"Without a good writing skill, you'll be doing yourself more harm than good."*

Reference.com puts it this way: "Writing is an important part of life, whether in the workplace or school, as a hobby or in personal communication. This skill helps the writer express feelings and thoughts to other people in a relatively permanent form" Writing skills as described by "Skillsyouneed.com" are an important part of communication. Good writing skills allow you to communicate your message with clarity and ease to a far larger audience than through face-to-face or telephone conversations.

As you can see, Writing is an essential part of our daily lives. There's hardly a day you'll not come across writing. Be it in the college, workplace, and conversation through the social media and so on.

Still Thinking of Writing? Here are 7 Reasons Why You Should: Expresses your personality

Writing allows you to express your thoughts and personal convictions. When you write, it demonstrates who you are as a person. Writing is a personality booster and shows your audience how you think or what you believe in. Reading this chapter, you should decipher that I'm encouraging you to acquire a writing skill and start writing.

Gives you Credibility

Writing makes it easy for your audience to believe in you and to relate with you. As a writer, the way you express your thoughts makes your audience see you as a credible person.

It makes them see you as someone who is intelligent and can be trusted. Even in colleges, good writers most at times get higher grades and are seen as more intelligent than their less literary counterparts.

Aids Networking

Writing travels farther than you, and makes it easy for your readers to want to associate with you. With a good writing skill, you will meet new people, go places, and have memorable experiences. Many popular writers in the world today, earned their reputation with writing. If you want to network with the right people today, start writing.

An Essential Job Skill

Employers place a high value on good writing skills. There is hardly any job today that doesn't require writing. You need to write a report, grant application or press release, exchange e-mails with your colleagues, and so on. You need a good writing skill to do that. Without one, you might not be able to get a job. It might even be difficult to get along with your colleagues (if you have any).

According to Grammarly, major companies spend upwards of US$3 billion (£1.8bn) per year training their employees to bring their writing abilities up to scratch.

It's a Profession

Writing is a profession. If you are a journalist or public relations professional, you need to start writing because it's your profession. For these professions, you need to write because that is what you do. Apart from these that traditionally need writing, other professions do too. If you dream to work as a professional in any of these fields, you need to write.

Means of Communication

Before the advent of the internet, many people used to communicate through the telephones. We can say then that it was easy to disregard writing. But today, writing has become the major means of communication among persons, businesses and organizations.

With emails, notes, tweets, texts and so on. It's hard for you to communicate without writing.

Communicating via these platforms can hinder or boost your career, relationship, and networking. Remember, good writing leads to good communication.

You Can Make a Living Writing

Of course, you can make a living writing, and affect many lives positively. Many writers, bloggers, freelancers, internet marketers, ghost writers and so on earn a decent income just by writing. Some writers and bloggers even make six figures and more monthly.

It's not a day's job but with effort, perseverance and persistence you'll too. And the most interesting part is that, making a living from writing gives you the freedom to continue earning forever.

Why not Sidestep Your Fears?

"It always seems impossible until it's done." says Nelson Mandela. It's always difficult to start, easy to procrastinate, and easier to dream of becoming a writer. Why not sidestep your fears today, ignite your passion and follow it up with actions. You will become a writer who will enjoy these and more.

Question

What other reasons do you have for choosing to become a writer? And what are the fears you have?

Activity

Identify five fears that you have about writing/freelance writing. Jot them down somewhere, and start working on them.

Chapter 2

Taking Actions: The Newbie Writer's Guide to Success

Having a writing skill isn't enough, there's one more important attitude you need to imbibe to succeed as a writer. In this chapter, I will take you through this to enhance your enthusiasm about writing. As an onlooker, you've always admired great writers in your field. You have read blog posts, newsletters, and e-books on how to get started as a writer. You even joined writing e-courses that take you through the nitty-gritty of writing. You're also a daily visitor to some of the popular blogging and writing websites in the world. You understand that writing is your calling. You respect writers and always wish to be called one.

You believe that writing as Paul Graham puts it doesn't just communicate ideas; it generates them, if you're bad at writing and don't like to do it, you will miss out on most of the ideas writing would have generated. Of course, great writers produce great ideas, and ideas rule the world

But, you're held up. Not only do you procrastinate beginning your writing career, you're also afraid of failure. The ideas are perfectly in your head, but you don't know how to get started. You have read that established writers make a lot of money writing, but you think you can't withstand their expertise.

Now take a look at this:

The Reality: Being in motion Vs. Taking Action

In his post, "The Mistake smart people make", James Clear aptly describes it thus: "Motion is when you're busy doing something, but the task will never produce an outcome by itself. Action on the other hand is the behavior that will get the result." Let's cite some examples:

- If I outline 30 ideas I want to write on, that's the motion. If I write and publish just an article, that's an action.

- I read a blog post on how to make money as a freelance writer, that's a motion. If I put it into practice and start making money, that's an action.
- If I study for a test, that's motion. If I take the test, that's an action.

Truth is, motion is good but action is better

I love the way Leonardo da Vinci puts it: "It had long since come to my attention that people of accomplishment rarely sat back and let things happen to them. They went out and happened to things."

Motion is good because it allows you to prepare, strategize and learn as a writer. But it will never produce a final result. Motion will show you the way but action will definitely take you there.

Are you Ready to take Actions?

As a newbie writer, you should understand that actions matter a lot. It is only when you take actions that you will succeed as a writer. It's the actions that established writers are taking that stand them out from the crowd. If you wish to be successful in your writing career, I advise you to do the following immediately in no particular order:

Start Small

Don't be in a hurry. Take calculated and important steps always. Simply put: begin with one task and get it completed before going to the next.

Reconnect with the Present Moment

Don't be in a hurry to make a name. There's always the euphoria and enthusiasm to break even as soon as you get started. Put those aside, remember that Rome was not built in a day.

Focus on how Instead of Ifs

What if's can really make you lose focus. Don't bother yourself with questions you might not have answers for. Instead of allowing your mind to get lost in what you don't have a control over, you should focus on how to get the job done.

Put the Distractions Away

These days, distractions are easy to come by. Our mobile devices are with us everywhere and it takes just a second to get distracted. You need to be wary of distractions as a writer, especially when you're writing. If it becomes so difficult, you can switch the gadgets off and put them away.

Utilize your Time Judiciously

Your time is an asset that you must guard jealously. Although you have no control over your time, but you do have control over the way you use it. Notwithstanding, you shouldn't harbour stress and tension about time, allow it to work towards your goals.

Stay Motivated

Make sure that you have some incentives to get self-motivated. Whenever you complete a writing task successfully, give yourself a pat on the back, and enjoy the moment. As a writer, the more motivated you are, the more actions you take.

Don't be a Perfectionist

This is an attitude bedeviling many beginner writers. As a rule, don't wait to be a perfect writer before you start writing. Write it anyhow, get criticized and become better. You should know that expertise is not attained in a day, it's learned on the job.

Never Follow the Majority

As a newbie writer, you need to figure out what makes you happy, what you can write on consistently over time, and follow it to the letter. Never follow the crowd because they're writing on a particular topic/ theme. At every point in time, don't be a copy-cat.

Be Enthusiastic

Enthusiasm is a great emotional state to be in, to be able to take actions. Be proud and happy to be called a writer. Tell whoever cares to listen that you're one. Flaunt the title on your social media platforms, let your family and friends know that, it's the path you have chosen.

The Time is Now

If indeed you want to take actions, there is no other time better to do that than now. Pick up your pen, sit in front of your computer, and begin your journey as a writer. Do not wait for the perfect moment, make this moment a perfect one.

ON A FINAL NOTE

Activity as John Wooden puts it should never be mistaken for achievement. If you want to be successful in your writing career, then you must begin to take actions. "Don't wait to be an expert before you take bold steps. Start something today, learn on the job, be determined and remain consistent. Indeed, expertise is earned over time and not a day's job."

Question

What has been hindering you from kick-starting your writing career?

Activity

Highlight five motions you have been taking so far, and convert them into actions.

Chapter 3

SO, You Want to Write? 10 Ways to Get Started

In my short stint as a professional freelance writer, I have received a lot of posers about how to get started as a writer. Some of these include:

Hey Shehu, I want to be a Writer. I love writing but it's difficult for me to start. What can I do?

Whenever I write, I feel my writing is not good, do you think so too?

I have written many articles in the past, but I am afraid to share it with the public, what's your advice on this?

And the list is endless.

During this period, I've come to realize that it's a problem that affects many who are passionate about writing, but simply don't know how to start. Let me tell you this: "While some believe that writers are born, others believe that they are made."

Irrespective of your belief, writing is an art that can be learnt and improved upon, when you follow the right steps and learn from great writers.

In this chapter, I will share a 10 step guide that can help your writing career, and make it easier for you to write despite the challenges you face.

The Hardest Part is Beginning

Writing is a herculean task I admit. It's always difficult to write and even more difficult to continue writing. But the hardest part of writing is the beginning. You should write regardless of whatever you're facing or the content you churn out at first. The most important thing is to write. "Good writers write regardless of the content". As soon as you begin writing, everything else will fall in place eventually.

Follow a Writing Process

As a writer, you should have a process which you follow. By this, I mean a routine that comes naturally, and not a step-by-step guide. Some of the processes most writers follow include the following:

- Pre-writing: This is where you find your idea, build on it, plan and structure it.
- Writing: This is the stage you write, concentrate more and avoid distractions. If possible, don't edit while writing
- Revision: At this stage, you add, remove, rearrange, rephrase and replace.
- Editing: This is the final stage before publishing.

When you follow these processes, writing becomes much easier and your contents are of more quality.

Read

Reading is important for writers. Good writers are avid readers. When you read, you equip yourself with the right words that can whet the appetite of your readers. As a writer, you need to find time to read always on a wide range of topics. Your reading should be extensive and not limited to a particular topic. When you inculcate the habit of reading as a writer, you'll become better.

Learn

Reading is necessary, but not enough for writers. As a writer, you need to learn too. Some of the things you'll learn about include the usage of grammar, how to write compelling sentences, punctuation, spelling, and so on. When you read, and complement it with learning, you are sure to super-charge the quality of your write-ups always.

Research

As a writer, you should always make a lot of research. Research helps your writing by making it more apt, qualitative, informative and factual. As a writer, your research should extend to topics that you have expertise in.

This helps to improve the quality of your content, and shows how deep your understanding of the topic is. So, whenever you want to write, research first.

Use Your Time Judiciously

If you seriously want to increase the quality of your write-up, then you should dedicate time to it. Without dedicating time to writing, it will be difficult to produce quality content.

This is because, writing is time-consuming, and the more time you spend on it the better. Many wannabe writers fail because they find it hard to find time to write. Find a time to write always.

Climb the Ladder

One thing you must know is that, when you write you shouldn't be keen on doing everything at once. Do not think you can start today, and be able to churn out thousands of words within a few hours. As a beginner, you need to start from somewhere depending on what works best for you. Start small and move up the ladder.

Practice

"Practice they say leads to perfection". You should practice writing always to become better. Never assume you can become a better writer without practicing. Practice daily with a few words, and see how far it'll go in improving you. You can start by writing 300, 500, and 750 words at least daily. Resources like 750 words, Twords and Daily Page will help you a lot with this.

Self-Motivation

When you motivate yourself, it helps you to write better. Lack of motivation is something that can hunt you as a writer. As a writer, the first step to motivating yourself is by sharing your writing with your readers, for appraisal and comments.

Doing this helps a lot, since you are sure someone out there is reading what you write. Likewise, you can do this in a negative way too. Whenever you write, remember that someone will learn and be motivated by what you do. But if you don't, your ideas will perish with you.

Be Disciplined

As a writer, you need to be disciplined to succeed. Without discipline, you'll not achieve your goals. With distractions on the social media, you must be disciplined to follow your routines and schedules. It's discipline that makes you to write when you have an interesting movie to watch, or an online hangout with your friends. When you are disciplined, you'll improve on your writing too.

ON A FINAL NOTE

In the world today, you cannot do without writing. Since it is a necessity, you must learn how to do it well. As it is said: "What is worth doing, is worth doing well". With these steps, be sure to see yourself writing quality content always.

Question

Which of these guides, do you practice the most, and how has it helped your writing career?

Activity

Identify three-five of these guides to start writing that you have just learnt. And start working on each of them immediately.

CHAPTER 4

The Best and Only Way to Learn Writing

One shocking fact I've realized over time about most people is that everyone wants to be a writer. In fact, I am yet to see a person who isn't interested in writing. Because everyone wants to write, many are bemused about where to start. They want to know the best way to learn writing.

Sometimes ago, I had an encounter with someone who read some of the posts on my blog. He was so enthusiastic and told me: *"Shehu, what are the secrets to writing."* To him, there are secrets writers hide from their audience.

A high school friend of mine once called me after a long time. At the end of our discussion he said: *"Shehu, I visited your blog days ago, and I am impressed by what you do. Though I find it easy to express myself in speech, it's always difficult for me to write."* **He confessed.**

These two encounters happened in a week. These and many more are questions I get from friends, family members, colleagues and followers of my blog.

Truth is, writing is both difficult and easy. Your perception to it matters and goes a long way in shaping you.

In this chapter, I hope to share with you the best and only one way to learn writing. But before that, let me make three shocking revelations:

You have no Excuses for not Writing

Whenever you are asked about writing and why you have not started. It's easy to bring up a thousand and one excuses. These excuses may include: lack of talent, inadequate writing resources, lack of mentors, the difficult nature of writing, inadequate time to write and so on. But do you think you can still write even when you have it all?

Peter elbow, while making his submission on this in his book, *"Writing without Teachers"*, aptly puts it thus:

People without education say, *"If only I had education I could write."* People with education say, *"If only I had talent, I could write."* People with education and talent say, "If only I had self-discipline I could write." *People with education, talent and self-discipline – and there are plenty of them who can't write – say, "If only ..." and don't know what to say next.* You can make excuses for not writing but there are none actually.

Writing is Your Right

It's your right to write, and it's only when you write that you can claim your right. Without writing, you'll lose your right to be right, but when you write you'll become right.

Abdullahi Muhammed in his book, *"Your Right To Write"* puts it this way:

"A lot of people are so scared to assert their right to write. I was scared too. Very much frightened. How could I call myself a writer? I had no Degree or certificate to show for it. I feared I could be challenged. That I was only pretending. That I was a serial impostor. Maybe you are, too. But in actual fact, you need no certification to write. It's a right you've always had ...your

birth right. If you write, you'll be right. Go a step further and author... that's how to become an authority. Whatever you conceive, and solemnly believe, you can achieve."

No Barriers to Writing

If there is any profession that gives everybody the freewill to do whatever they want, in the best way they can, irrespective of their backgrounds then writing comes first. There is no barrier to becoming a writer irrespective of your discipline. What matters most is your ability to learn how to write, and writing always.

Many great writers today, never studied Arts or Humanities in College or University. Studying these related courses is good, but not studying them isn't a barrier. I love the way Seth Godin puts it: "The biggest challenge is that there are no barriers. If you want to do it, go do it. Ideas worth spreading, spread." And I say: "If you want to write, just write. Ideas worth writing, write" Now, you know that:

- No barriers to writing

- Writing is your right
- You have no excuses for not writing.

Then, what's the best and only way to learn writing.

If I may ask you?

- What's the best way to learn how to walk? Walking, isn't it?
- What's the best way to learn how to speak? Speaking, right?
- What's the best way to learn how to cook? Cooking, am I correct?

So, the best and only way to learn writing is:

- Writing
- Writing, and
- Writing.

There are no two ways about it.

It is only when you write that you can master the art of writing.

Hear this

- If you read the best of books on writing
- Possess the best resources that can aid your writing career

- Subscribe to blogs that can make you a better writer
- Attend writing conferences to equip you better.

Do these actions make you a better writer? Absolutely No! The truth about writing is that, if you don't write, you are not a writer. If you want to learn writing, you need to write. Stop procrastination. Pick up your pen right now and write.

The first draft might look messy, but that's the best way to go. When you write, you learn and master it. But if you fail to write, you can never learn writing. Proficiency isn't what you need now. You need to start. When you start, you learn and become better.

ON A FINAL NOTE

Writing is a daunting, time-consuming and lonely task. But if you wish to learn it, you need to start writing. It's only when you write, that you can be called a writer. When you write, you claim your right. When you author, you become an authority.

Question

What are the fears you have about writing? How has writing made you a better writer?

Activity

Write a short essay (Minimum 500 words) about the fears you have about writing.

CHAPTER 5

Eager to Begin a Freelance Writing Career? 5 Things you Must Know

As a newbie, the word freelance might seem odd to you. Never worry, I'll do justice to that in a jiffy. Now let's go deep into some definitions: Study.com, in one of its articles opined that: "The word 'freelance' itself comes from the Middle Ages, to describe the knights who would defend whichever king paid them, rather than being loyal to just one king. These knights were referred to as 'free lanced'."

In a nutshell, loyalty is alien to freelancing. Freelance according to the Business Dictionary is a term which means working on a contract basis for a variety of companies, as opposed to working as an employee for a single company. From this definition, it's clear that when you say someone freelances, it means that he/ she isn't tied to a particular firm, company or contract.

Similarly, according to freelancer.com "Freelancing has become a popular professional choice lately". It continues thus: "Freelancing comes with its plentiful perks. Be it choosing your own working schedule and hours, to deciding on establishing a practice which is full-time or part-time, the choices are plenty". So, has freelancing finally come to stay? What are the statistics of freelancers in the world today? Now take a look at the following: According to the Freelancers' Union, there are 53 million people in the US doing freelance work. 34% of the national workforce! Likewise, people who freelance contribute $715 billion in freelance earning to the economy. That's a lot.

In the UK, it's revealed that the freelance economy has grown by 14% in the past decade, and there are 1.4 million British freelancers across different sectors of the economy. Not bad too. According to a report by the freelance job site Elance, the number of businesses hiring freelance writers online increased by 46% in

2013. In Europe, freelancing is also soaring. A report titled: "Future Working: The Rise of Europe's Independent Professionals", indicates that Freelancers are the fastest growing group in the EU labor market as their numbers have increased by 45% from just under 6.2 million to 8.9 million in 2013.

What Do You Observe?

The freelance industry is growing and becoming an acceptable profession. Freelance writing, the backbone of online marketing accounts for about 18% of the freelance jobs online.

These statistics impress many wannabe freelance writers, who are motivated to start a career of their own. While some started and along the line, found the career stressful, and called it quits, others are afraid of starting and satisfied with discussing the industry trends without getting engaged. Whichever group you belong to:

Listen to this:

Many who could have succeeded in freelance writing are afraid of failure, others who damned the consequence to begin, are doing it the wrong way. Freelance writing offers you a unique opportunity to showcase your skills and get rewarded. However, it could discourage and frustrate you if not done with the right mind-set.

In this chapter, I will share some tips on how you can successfully kick-start your career in the industry, and see yourself smiling at the end of the day

Start Anyhow

Yes, you read that right. If you desire to succeed in this career, you have to take actions. One of the greatest harms to yourself and career is to continue waiting for the best time and opportunity. The truth is that, these may never come, and at the end of the day you'll continue in the same cycle. "There's magic in action", and you have to take the bold steps whether you think you're ready for it or not.

By starting anyhow, I do not mean that you should offer your services at ridiculous prices. It means that despite the challenges you face, you need to do something immediately. When you start, opportunities will knock at your door. The whole world will recognize and appreciate you for what you do, and with time you'll get the desired results.

Create a Brand

Has it ever struck you that, you are the number one brand for your business? Are you proud to tell people, anywhere and anytime about what you do? You need to identify that, this is a profession and you must treat it as such. You must identify why you are in the business in the first place, and improve yourself too.

Some of the things you must put in place to brand yourself as a freelance writer include:

- A functional blog/ website
- A captivating profile on various social media platforms such as Facebook, Twitter, Instagram, LinkedIn etc.

- A facebook page to promote your business and services.
- Offline meetings / Seminars etc.

These platforms should indicate what you do. When you put these in place, you need to reach out to your target audience and spread the message to them too.

Build Social Proof

The online business is populated and it takes a lot of time to get into the hearts of your potential audience. So as a freelance writer who's just starting, you need to establish yourself to earn people's trust.

So what do you do?

You need Social Proof.

Now, you might wonder what the heck this is all about.

In simple terms, **Social Proof is the act of having a reputation online in your chosen niche or career.**

To simplify this: Quickly run a Google search for your name, and see what pops up in the search results.

What do you see?

Your Facebook profile, Twitter, LinkedIn etc. Well, if it's so, that's what the web has about you in its records. Don't be surprised, some will not display any result at all. Again do this: Run a search of my name: *AbdulGaniy Shehu*, and what do you find?

The result is glaring, isn't it? Okay, let's do this too: search for *Bamidele Onibalusi*, and observe the difference with mine. The difference as you see it, is what is referred to as Social Proof.

Therefore, if you want to start and eventually succeed in freelance writing, you need to establish a social proof, and show potential clients they are dealing with a real person. Now, you might ask, how do you establish Social Proof and become successful at it. My response: There are quite a lot of ways to achieve this. In the meantime, your writer website which I'm sure you already have in place, or plan to have can serve that purpose.

Remain Consistent

When it comes to any online/ offline business, consistency matters a lot, and separates doers from dreamers. If you think of starting your freelance writing career, you should be ready to be consistent. With consistency:

- You're committed to your blog and make regular updates too.
- You follow up on clients despite repeated failures.
- You follow up on different social media platforms, interacting with clients.
- You are sure of achieving your freelance writing goals.

A story I wish to share with you about this, is that of one of my mentors in writing. Within 3 years, he was consistent and focused, and today he earns six figures (In dollars), annually from freelance writing.

Are you surprised?

Okay, how did he achieve that?

This young man, as a university undergraduate founded a website to announce essay contests and also share tips on writing with fellow writers in his country. He did this consistently, till he discovered the goldmine in Affiliate marketing, which he quickly keyed into, organizing e-courses for his audience. He never called it quits, until he found out that he can earn more through freelance writing, which he started by creating another website for this purpose.

Today the rest is history, he's been featured on various international platforms such as Jewish Journal, Huffington Post, Entrepreneur magazine, Inc. Magazine, Forbes, USA TODAY and a host of others. The truth is that, he couldn't have achieved all these without been consistent and persistent. He faced challenges, but today he's a success, and a story worthy of sharing with you.

Distinguish Yourself

As a freelance writer, you need to distinguish yourself from others to succeed. You should bring in that unique factor that will make you stand out, and become the writer of first choice. If you can do this, then you are close to your dreams.

Jon Morrow of Smart Blogger is known for his long articles, and he does it so well. Bamidele Onibalusi of Writers in Charge is also known for this, though he does it in a different way and style. Carol Tice of Make a living writing, curated the idea of paying freelance writers who get published on her blog, and that aids the contents on her platform greatly. Other writers are doing different things to succeed in this regard. That distinguishing factor will make you stand out and stand the test of time.

On a Final note

This is 2018, and freelance writing will continue to serve the interests of many as long as online marketing and business exist. Don't you think it's time to sidestep your fears, and grab this opportunity? Are you still afraid of taking that bold step of becoming the next big freelance writer, the world has been waiting for?

Question

What are your fears about freelance writing? Are you ready to begin today?

Activity

If you have not started. Create the platforms that you need for your freelance writing career. The most important ones being the Writer Website, Social Media Platforms (LinkedIn and Twitter) especially.

CHAPTER 6

10 Successful Tips for Beginner Freelance Writers

Freelancing has played a major role in the economy of countries and individuals over the years. There have been milestones attained, and breakthroughs in previous years. 2018 won't be an exception. Freelance writing will continue to soar as I revealed in the last chapter.

As a newbie freelance writer, you might wonder what should be put in place to enable you compete favourably in this ever dynamic and demanding market. In this chapter, I'll share with you ten (10) tips for a successful career in freelance writing.

Start From Somewhere

"Little drops of water make a mighty ocean". Starting your career as a newbie in the freelance writing industry requires that you start small and then climb the success ladder. When starting, do not compare yourself with experts in the industry, they started somewhere too. Approach small businesses, start by writing for small online publications, and volunteer to do some work. When you start small, you can measure your progress and success too.

So, start small and achieve big.

Pick a Niche

What is a niche? You might ask. A niche is your area of specialization as a freelance writer. This is the area you're known for, and clients can vouch for your expertise on it too. Okay, to simplify it:

On my blog, where I teach about writing and freelance writing. This shows that my blogging niche is writing and freelance writing isn't it? That is why I can't publish posts on Music, Politics, News and so on, on the blog, because they are not my blog niches. In the same way, as a freelance writer, you should have a niche to succeed. With a niche, you are good to go.

Remain Focused

Let me tell you something frankly. Freelance writing is difficult. It's difficult to get clients. After getting clients, writing is an arduous task.

After taking your time to write, clients might reject your works, and I can go on. So, imagine yourself continuing in this cycle for the next few months, what happens? You will be dejected and frustrated. You might even quit. This is where focus comes in. You should motivate yourself and also be patient too. I assure you that, with focus you will go places in this industry.

Be Professional

"Freelance writing is a business and not a hobby". This is the mind-set and attitude all beginner freelance writers should have. If you wish to achieve your goals, do not take freelance writing, as a hobby. Professionalism is key, in your dealings with your clients.

As a professional you should:

- Ask clients about the specifics of their jobs.

- Do the work diligently and on time
- Respond to emails and queries.
- Offer valuable advice to clients.

Of course, professionalism pays in the long run.

Consider guest posting

As a newbie freelance writer, you are not known to potential clients. So, what do you do? You might be wondering. Although there are many ways to put yourself out there as a freelance writer. One effective and easy way to go about this, is to write posts targeted at your niche (which I mentioned earlier), for blogs, online publications, magazines etc. I hope you now understand, what guest posting is all about?

Although it might not be easy to get in to top publications at first, but starting with the small ones, will get you there. Guest posting gives you social proof, and with time, you become an authority too. Do you see yourself as an authority? Start guest posting.

Start a Blog

Blogging is an underutilized tool by most freelance writers. With a blog, you get to write consistently about a particular area of interest. Now what is the purpose of a blog?

- It gives you a platform.
- It gives you social proof.
- It makes you an authority.
- Your audience are potential clients.
- It provides a potential income stream for you.

I strongly recommend that you start a blog as a freelance writer (though it's not compulsory). Start a blog and build a name in the industry.

Improve Your Writing Ability

As a freelance writer, your most important asset is your writing skill and ability. Therefore, you should develop this skill regularly. With a good writing ability, you can take on different writing projects.

When you develop your writing ability, you can diversify your income, and become irresistible to clients. You can learn e-Book writing/ formatting, white papers, content marketing and so on, by visiting blogs, reading books, and following websites too.

Develop your writing ability on a daily basis, and you will be better off for it.

Increase Your Online Visibility

The world today is on the internet, and everything is done on the go. As a freelance writer, you must key into this, and develop your online visibility. The whole world should know what you offer, and how that can change their businesses. You should be visible on social media platforms such as Facebook, Twitter, LinkedIn, Instagram, About.me, and so on. Likewise, you should be consistent and purposeful with your content and posts on these platforms. Online visibility is the order of the day in businesses, and you should utilise it.

Diversify Your Earnings

Freelance writing offers you a consistent income if done the right way. But to succeed in the industry, you must diversify your earnings. As a freelance writer, you can go into blogging, affiliate marketing, eBook publishing, and other online businesses. With multiple streams of income, you can be sure of decent earnings through various means. If you want to earn more, diversify your earnings.

Do it Afraid

Writers generally are afraid (This includes the experts too). Some of the fears writers have are:
- Who will read my articles?
- My writings are awful.
- Everybody writes better than I do.
- Can I ever make money from writing? And so on.

Some of these fears are true, but many writers have gone ahead to achieve their respective goals despite them. As a freelance writer, these fears are also existent. Some of the fears of freelance writers include:

- Can I ever get clients?
- If I ever get clients, can I impress them to accept my works?
- Will I be able to earn consistently from freelance writing?

Of course, these fears exist but should they scare you from beginning your career as a freelance writer? No. Rather, they should spur you to take actions and succeed in your chosen career. So, friend, do it afraid and rule the world

ON A FINAL NOTE

Actions separate doers from dreamers. Your freelance writing career in previous years might not have ended on a good note, but that is not the end of the world.

This year offers you a unique opportunity to make the changes you want, and achieve your dreams. It is not too late to make hay, after all the sun still shines.

Question

What other things do you think fellow freelance writers should do to achieve success in freelance writing?

Activity

Have you started a blog? If no, try to create one and start immediately.

CHAPTER 7

Top 10 Challenges of A Beginner Freelance Writer (And How to Overcome Them)

To be honest, your journey as a beginner freelance writer hasn't been rosy. This was never what you expected. Freelance writing is over-hyped, you think. In fact, it's hard to make money from freelance writing, you insist. This is because getting a job as a freelance writer has been a herculean task, so far.

The picture painted above is what an average beginner freelance writer faces daily. But you also need to ask that in spite of these challenges: Why is the freelance economy the order of the day for businesses? Why is it that, about 54 million Americans are Freelancers? You read that right? It is even projected that 40% of Americans will embrace the freelance economy by 2020.

The Bitter Truth

Freelance writing seems easy from the outside. But those who have been a part of this growing field know that this is far from the truth. The prospect of freelance writing is high, but it takes targeted efforts, careful strategy and skills to be successful at it. Beginner freelance writers face challenges. No doubt, are these challenges exclusive to freelance writers alone? No. Is it possible to scale through these challenges? Yes. What can I do to overcome these challenges? Read on

In this chapter, I will reveal the top 10 challenges faced by beginner freelance writers, and what to do to overcome each of them.

The Beginner's Mind-set

As a newbie freelance writer, the first challenge you face is the beginner's mind-set. Having read about this emerging market, you can't wait to succeed as one.

You're in a haste to succeed, but something keeps telling you that, you are a beginner. Then you are tempted to write for content mills, write free samples and accept low paying gigs to gain experience. You do not believe in yourself anymore. You are afraid to get in touch with editors to feature you on their platforms for social proof.

What to do: Ponder over this. An engineer who just graduated from college and starts working immediately, does this make him or her different from other experienced engineers? Yes. But will this make him or her stoop so low not to be paid for the job they have done? No. Of course, you can't compare yourself with established writers. But this does not mean you should belittle yourself and earn so low. Remember, it is a business, so be yourself and improve yourself.

Competition

One of the toughest challenge you will face as a beginner freelance writer is competition. The freelance writing world is populated with a pool of qualified and experienced writers competing with one another. If you allow the competition to get into your head, you might feel dejected, and even lose hope in your ability.

What to do: Don't compare yourself with anybody. If you should ever compete, it should be with yourself. Always make sure you are qualified for a gig, before applying for it. There will always be competition, but if you are competent and able to show your potential clients that you can deliver, you will get there.

Social Pressure

Till date, it's difficult for most freelance writers to identify themselves with the profession. Is freelance writing a career? Many freelance writers are asked many times. One undeniable fact is that the social pressure of being a freelance writer is huge. This is so because the idea people have about a career is different from what you do. To most, before you can be said to have a career, you should leave home by 9am, and arrive by 5pm on weekdays.

What to do: This has to do with the perception people have about the freelance writing career. To most it's unbelievable. (How can a person stay at home, punching the keyboard always, say he's earning 4-5 figures in dollars monthly?) As a freelance writer, forget whatever anybody says. Focus on the job at hand, and be bold to introduce yourself as one to anyone who cares to listen.

Social Proof

Social proof as I stated in the previous chapter, is so important for any freelance writer to succeed. What's Social proof you may ask? It's the practice of writing on popular platforms in your niche to showcase your expertise to your audience and potential clients.

Why is it so important? The freelance writing business is mostly online and it's difficult for clients to trust someone whose abilities have not been tested.

Where can I publish my articles for Social proof? On any blog or website, as far as it is relevant to your niche. Some of the top platforms freelance writers publish on include: Forbes, Huffington Post, Business Magazine, Entrepreneur Magazine, Fast Company, and the list is endless. Getting social proof is essential for you as a freelance writer, but it's a challenge for most beginners.
What to do:
- As a beginner, you should realise that it's difficult for top editors to accept you to write for them. You need to show them you're capable.
- Start by writing guest posts for less authority blogs in your niche. Some of these include LinkedIn pulse, Medium.com, Thrive Global, and so on.
- You can showcase these guest posts to top editors as your experience, and pitch them to write for their platforms.

- Never make the mistake of sending your pitch to a general e-mail or contact form (That's a recipe for failure).
- Check the platform, read their guidelines, check out for the editor's e-mail and send an irresistible pitch.

It might prove difficult when you start, but with dedication and hard-work, you'll get in.

Getting high-Paying Clients

What's the essence of freelance writing, if you cannot get high paying clients? Many freelance writers accept and write for content mills (That pay peanuts despite considerable efforts from them). Writers are special and talented, and should be treated fine. If you truly want to make it as a freelance writer, you should go the hard-way of getting real clients that value what you do. It is a challenge (I faced same too)

What to do: Getting high paying clients is difficult, but it's worth it. You need to put in more efforts both on the Social Media platforms

(Such as Twitter and LinkedIn especially), and through other means by cold pitching.

Face Rejection

Many times, you send a wonderful pitch to a top website in your niche, and it gets rejected. Sometimes, you send hundreds of cold pitches to potential clients without getting responses even after several follow-ups. No doubt you will face rejections as a beginner freelance writer.

What to do:
- Develop a thick skin for these rejections (Accept them as they come and move on)
- Hang out with fellow freelance writers on various groups online, and discuss some of these challenges with them.
- Remember: A problem discussed is half solved.

Lack of Ideas

A freelance writer must never be short of ideas. How do you develop an idea for a pitch you want to write for a website that pays? How do you come up with article ideas? It's difficult not to run out of ideas, but it's easy to get fresh ideas always if you are ready.

What to do:
- As a freelance writer, you must be an avid reader
- Read anything that comes your way from Facebook, Twitter, and LinkedIn updates
- Read blog posts, novels, educational materials and so on
- When you read wide, there will always be something to write.
- When reading updates and blog posts, read the comments too. It gives you an idea of the challenges people are facing and an idea of a solution you can offer too.

Running a business

Approaching freelance writing like a typical business is a challenge most beginner freelance writers face. If you do not treat freelance writing as a business, then you are doing yourself more harm than good. You should be able to evaluate where you are coming from, where you are, and the future prospects. A beginner freelance writer will find this difficult.

What to do: In treating freelance writing as a business, you must take one step at a time. Start by having a daily recap of what you have achieved. Then, you could have weekly and monthly recaps too. Some of the basic things you should always include in your reports include:
- The number of articles you have written for your blog
- The number of guest posts that have been published
- The companies you sent cold pitches to
- The rate of response.
- Your income reports (when you make money).

When you measure your progress, you stay motivated and want to do more.

Remaining Productive

Productivity matters to freelance writers. When you are productive, you remain on top of your game. It's difficult to stay productive, as sometimes you can't just help it. You could lose focus and may want to quit.

What to do:
- Evaluate your lifestyle (How well do you sleep, and how healthy are you?)
- Exercise regularly (This helps your mind to relax)
- Eat good food (do not consume junks and the likes)
- Invest your time in reading personal development blogs.
- Find out time to hang out with friends
- Join conversations online and offline
- Watch a favorite movie/ show on TV, and your favorite team playing too.

These will ease the pressure and stress of the work on you. It keeps you mentally and physically healthy. And ensure you stay productive always.

Uncertainty

The uncertain nature of freelance writing scares people away from it. It is possible to have a lot of clients today, and they could disappear for months. This happens to everybody. So, how is it possible not to stay out of jobs?

What to do:
- Write as many guest posts as possible for blogs in your niche (With this, businesses will find you).
- Stamp your authority by contributing regularly on business websites such as Forbes, Entrepreneur Magazine, and Inc. magazine, and so on.
- Do not be too lazy to look for clients and pitch always.
- Apart from cold-pitching, use the Twitter and LinkedIn alternatives to get prospective clients.

- Write and monetize e-book(s) for your audience through your blog, Kindle, Create Space, and so on.
- Start a course that solves problems on a topical issue and earn through it.
- Consider blogging and making money through affiliate marketing.

With these, you are sure of making more money as a freelance writer. There you have it. All freelance writers face these challenges, but beginners face them more. The experts who earn 4-5 figures in dollars monthly, have faced same too. As a beginner, when you face these challenges, do not be afraid and never lose hope. Remember: "When the going gets tough, the tough keeps going".

Question

Which of these challenges do you face as a freelance writer, and how are you able to overcome them?

Activity

Have you started treating Freelance Writing as a Business? If no, start doing so with the tips provided in this chapter.

CHAPTER 8

7 Daily Productivity Hacks for Freelance Writers

As a freelance writer, your day is a busy one. You have to write articles for your blog (If you have any), you need to deliver clients' work on time, social media campaign is also there, you need to guest post, improve your social proof, and so on. But the truth is that, you have just 24 hours to take these actions. You're always overwhelmed with work, to the point that you regret the day you joined the freelance writing world. Today, that is over.

In this chapter, I'll take you through productivity hacks that can supercharge your performance as a freelance writer. With these daily productivity hacks, your day as a freelance writer will never be the same again.

The earlier the better

You need to start writing early as a freelance writer. This is because it gives you the best output always. Research has shown that, creativity peaks in the morning, as the creative connections in our brains are most active then. The early morning is the ideal time for you to generate new thoughts and ideas. If you wish to be more creative daily as a freelance writer, you need to consider this. Wake up early, and start writing.

Set Out a Roadmap

A roadmap gives you a breakdown of what to write in an article. This could be breaking your write-up into the drafting, first, second and the redrafting stages. Without a roadmap, your writing will not flow, and you'll be less productive. You will be doing everything at a time. Writing, jotting down points, and editing (All at the same time!). With a clear writing roadmap, you know what to write, how to write, where and when to write. Remember, he who fails to plan, plans to fail.

Just write

As easy as this seems, it is the most difficult task for freelance writers (Yours sincerely, inclusive). It is difficult to write, and focus on it alone. You want to multitask (Social media campaigns, Research, and pitching clients) at the same time. But a 2009 Unanimous Stanford University research *found out that people who chronically multitask show an enormous range of deficits. They're basically terrible at all sorts of cognitive tasks.* If you want to surcharge your daily productivity as a freelance writer, ditch other activities when writing, and just write.

You're good, be better

Have you observed that your writing speed determines the number of words you write daily? As a freelance writer, you need to up your typing skills, if you want a productive day. You might have all the great ideas in your head, but if you suck at typing, it will affect your output. If you type about 30 words per minute presently, you need to work harder to raise it to about 60 words per minute and improve from there.

Take breaks

Writing is a lonely and arduous task. Imagine yourself sitting down all day in front of the computer, and doing nothing but writing or typing. In some hours, you will be worked out, and might be experiencing eye strains. When this happens, the best thing to do is to take breaks. Walk away from your computer, go play with your buddies around, your kids/wife (if you do have), take snacks to freshen up and then go back to work.

According to Fast Company, breaks must be prioritized at work because they keep us from getting bored, help us retain information and re-evaluate our goals. Take a break while writing, it aids productivity.

Adequate sleep aids a lot

Sleep deprivation is something you need to look into if you want to remain productive as a freelance writer. The National Sleep Foundation in 2015, recommended an average of 7-8 hours of sleep per day for an adult. You need to ask yourself, how much sleep do I take daily? Arianna Huffington in her book, "The Sleep Revolution" opines that we are in the midst of a sleep deprivation crisis, which has profound consequences – on our health, job performance, relationships and happiness. Sleep well and you will transform your freelance writing career one night at a time.

Prayer

Prayer, as it is said is the key. It helps create a focus in you for the day. No matter what religious beliefs you hold, don't forget to pray before you get your day started. With prayer, you're able to overcome mental blocks that could hinder your progress during the day. The grace of God cannot be over-emphasized too. So pray, and figure out how it will aid your productivity.

On a Final note

Your daily productivity matters a lot as a freelance writer. When you fail at this, your freelance writing career is adversely affected. With these hacks, your productivity as a freelance writer will sprout. Don't just go through them, take actions and quadruple your productivity.

Question

Which of these productivity hacks do you use the most, and what experience do you have with them?

Activity

Try to implement one of these productivity hacks, and see how it works. For example, start by writing early in the morning, and see how far you'll go.

CHAPTER 9

10 Social Media Productivity Hacks for Freelance Writers

With more than 2 billion people having social media accounts across the globe, the social media is here to stay and will remain a market with a lot of potential. While this large number of social media accounts is encouraging, it's a scary one for many freelance writers.

Scary?

Yes, we live in a world where according to the AdWeek, 41% of online time is spent on social media. This means that most activities of many people are only limited to the social media alone.

As a freelance writer, it provides a great opportunity for you, if you can use it well. That's it – you need to know the social media productivity hacks for freelance writers.

Not trying to sound too pessimistic.

As a freelance writer, your productivity on the social media is on the line if you can't ask yourself these questions: How productive are the long periods of time spent on the social media? How easy is it to stay productive on the social media as a freelance writer? Are there any tricks that could aid your productivity even when you share updates on various social media platforms? Can the social media be a great avenue to attract more clients?

How can you build relationships on social media that can surcharge your earnings? Well, here are the answers.

10 Social Media Productivity Hacks for Freelance Writers

Believe it or not, the reality is that if you do not plan your social media activities well, you will not only regret it but see that your time is spent doing nothing. With these productivity hacks, your presence as a freelance writer on the social media will never be the same.

Map out a strategy

The Social media is a place that needs a lot of plans to succeed. As a freelance writer, you need to map out a strategy that fits what you offer. For instance, if you are a Tech specialist; you should map out strategies in this line. Test your Strength, Weakness, Opportunity, and Threat. Your strategy should include when you want to post, the platforms you want to use, and the groups you want to follow, and so on.

With a good strategy in place, you will able to promote your work, land well-paying clients, and your productivity will soar higher.

Figure out who you want to follow

The greatest mistake you can make as a freelance writer on the social media is not following the right set of people. You should not follow everybody; only follow those that matter to your business. Following the right set of people means identifying influencers in your niche, who could aid your career.

This involves finding out the social media platforms where your fellow freelance writers hang out and socialize, and join them too.

In addition, you should follow writing blogs/ websites that share what you do often and motivate you to become better at it too.

Build One-to-One Relationships

Relationship matters. In fact, social media relationships matter to you as a freelance writer. In building a relationship, you should:

- **Reveal your identity:** As a freelance writer, you should display your profile picture on your platforms. This gives potential clients a sense that you are human, and not a robot.
- **Be friendly:** You should be friendly in your interactions with fellow users, and treat them in a likable manner (like, and share their comments). It goes a long way to making your relationship grow.

As a freelance writer, the relationships you build matters and aid your productivity.

Be Smart

There are many discussions happening on the social media on a daily basis. As a freelance writer, content matters a lot to you. (You need this to post regularly on your blog, and also write quality content for your clients always).

The social media platforms offer a great avenue to get ideas for your content. This does not mean that you are plagiarizing other peoples' work or being lazy to research. Rather it saves you a lot of time, and makes your contents reader-friendly, and trending.

Most discussions on the social media platforms are avenues for the freelance writer to tap from. Be smart, and your productivity will soar higher than you have ever imagined.

Re-Use Content

Have you ever come across a content that has thousands of likes and shares on Facebook and Instagram? If you have, then that's an untapped goldmine for a freelance writer.

Content like this can be re-used to fit in what you intend to write for your clients or as a guest post. It's through these social media platforms that the level of engagement of a particular post can be measured.

After all, you can't compare a post having a thousand likes, with another having just ten likes. The same way a post that got shared by users multiple times can't be compared with that of fewer shares. While using the social media as a freelance writer, take a look at some of the popular posts, re-use the content for your purpose, and see the results you will get.

Plan Your Time

It's said that: "He who fails to plan, plans to fail." The recipe for failure on the social media is not planning your time.

To stay productive, you must plan your time well. Evaluate the various social media platforms, as well as the time and activities you want to carry out on each. Do not engage yourself in unnecessary chats, comments and hang-outs that will not aid your productivity. Remember you only have 24 hours in a day to complete your assignments. Make the best use of them.

Be Disciplined

Imagine yourself in a situation, whereby you have a guest post to send to a top blog in your niche, the deadline for a client's work is knocking at the door, and you still want to reach out to more clients. Then suddenly an old buddy of yours got in touch with you via one of the social media platforms. What do you do? Truth is, most people will be distracted and would have totally forgotten the tasks at hand. As a freelance writer, your productivity on the social media is directly proportional to your discipline.

If you are not disciplined, you will not be productive. Always be disciplined, know when to socialize, comment, reach out to more clients, and perform your various tasks. With discipline, you will be productive.

Be Selective

Many freelance writers make the mistake of wanting to belong to all social media platforms they can find out there. This is both unproductive and time-consuming. There are lots of social media platforms in the world today, and you can't be everywhere at the same time. You should choose and use the right social media platform unique to you and productive for your business.

When you streamline the platforms you sign up to, it will go a long way to aid your productivity.

Schedule and Monitor Updates

No matter how much you try, it will be difficult to catch up with the discussions on the various platforms and monitor them, combined with your freelance writing activities. To make things easier, you need to schedule and monitor updates with the necessary tools. Some of these tools such as Hootsuite enable you to share various updates across many platforms at different times.

All you need to do is to schedule the updates, and everything will move on fine. You should monitor the updates, by checking out who is following you, who liked your page, the number of views your profile has garnered and lots more.

This helps to keep you on track as you are sure of the impacts your activities on the social media are having.

Be Patient

As a freelance writer, you should never be in haste to achieve results. Results will come, though it takes time, hard-work and dedication. In fact, sometimes you will carry out some of these activities, and yet not get the results at the beginning. If you do, you might be forced to quit, and that will be the end of your freelance writing career.

With patience, you will see how productive these activities will be at the end.

On a Final Note

The social media provides a lot of opportunities for freelance writers. It helps you reach out to more clients, build more relationships, and have a feel of what people are discussing.

But if you do not use the social media platforms well, they will distract and make you unproductive.

As a freelance writer, you have to maintain a balance between your social activities and your business. With these hacks, your activities on the social media will make you surcharge your productivity daily.

Question

Do you think the social media is distracting to freelance writers?

Which of these productivity hacks do you think can aid you to stay on track in your business as a freelance writer?

Activity

Have you mapped out a strategy yet for your social media platforms? If no, do so immediately.

CHAPTER 10

Dealing with Procrastination as a Freelance Writer: A Personal Experience

It was late 2016. For 42 days I didn't post a new article on my blog. I stopped my freelance writing activities which affected my blog updates too. It was a hell of a time, an unforgettable experience and moment of deep reflection worth sharing with you.

What happened?

Shortly before my convocation ceremony (Which came up in October 2016), a friend invited me over to carry out a particular task that will last for some weeks. This, I agreed to reluctantly and together we carried out this task for two weeks. While this task lasted, I wrote nothing either on my blog or elsewhere. My writing career suffered a huge setback.

As if that was not enough

Before commencing the task with my friend, my laptop's battery got damaged. And with the electricity challenges in my country, I couldn't help the situation. Immediately after the task, I became so reluctant to pick up my pen again. I wasn't eager to type on my computer, and whenever each day passes by, I always assure myself that I would write the next day.

The monster called Procrastination

Procrastination, which means postponing, or setting aside a task you ought to execute today for another day is a monster. It's the killer of dreams and an effective way to stop pursuing a particular cause. When you procrastinate you become so lazy. You develop a psychological apathy towards the task at hand, and most times you dread ever going back to it.

Procrastination for a writer: My Personal Experience

Procrastination affects writing just like other professions. In fact, that of a writer is obviously detrimental. During that period, I lost my writing voice. It made writing so difficult, and I dreaded ever putting anything down to write. My writing became so disrupted that the only consolation I put up for myself is that I will write tomorrow.

In fact, I wondered if I could ever be able to write again. That is what procrastination does for a writer. It makes you lose your self-confidence, you cease to believe in your abilities, and instead of being a writer you become a waiter.

How to Deal with Procrastination as a Writer

Procrastination affected my writing career, but I learnt some lessons especially on how to handle it. This is to prevent a repeat, and make sure that you don't make the same mistakes as mine.

So, here are 5 ways to deal with procrastination as a writer:

Understand the Phenomenon

The first step to dealing with procrastination is to understand the phenomenon and how it works. Always have it in mind that it creeps into your career unknowingly. It gives you a sense of confidence that nothing will happen if you fail to write today. As a writer, when you have this feeling, you should understand that it's procrastination. So, act fast.

Write Daily

This is an advice that expert writers tell beginner writers to heed. When you write daily, you achieve many things. Here are some of them:

- You remain in a right state of mind to write (This is because writing deals with your state of mind)
- You remain less bothered about what to post
- You have a large pool of ready articles to choose from.

With a daily writing time table, you will have defeated procrastination by a large percentage.

Make writing a top priority

You cannot write daily if you don't make writing an important aspect of your life. Essentially, you should think, dream and feel writing. It's only when writing becomes a top priority that you won't think of anything else than to write.

In reality, you could execute other tasks as well but writing should remain top most in your heart. With this mind-set, you won't see yourself delaying a writing task for another time or day.

Make reading a habit

Good writers are avid readers, and avid readers never run out of writing ideas. To deal with procrastination, you must make it a habit to read always.

- Read novels as much as you can.
- Read about writing and its different techniques.
- Read about the challenges faced by writers and how they overcome them.
- Read blog posts of fellow writers, top players in the writing industry, mentors, and so on.

With these you will remain on top of your game always, and write as much as you can.

Think About Your Audience

Thinking about your audience is an effective way to handle procrastination. As a writer, your audience is an important aspect of your career. Not only do they read what you write, they wait for it, and put it into action. Now, imagine a scenario where your audience feels disappointed because you didn't show up. Devastating isn't it?

You might as well lose a sizeable number of readers if this persists for long. The internet is so populated, and you need fresh content always to stay on top of the game. As a writer, when you think about the audience, you will never procrastinate. Rather you would want to satisfy them always.

On a Final Note

Procrastination is real, and it's a cog in the wheel of a writer's progress. The surprising thing is that it creeps unknowingly into a writer's career, and if not taken care of, will cause a huge damage to it. As a writer, you should always be ready for setbacks, disappointments and so on in your career.

They weigh you down and make you want to think that procrastination is the next thing for you. With the practical steps highlighted above, you will overcome procrastination and be in charge of your writing career once again.

Question

As a writer, have you ever experienced procrastination? What are the steps you took to overcome it successfully?

Activity

Start writing daily. You can begin with 250 words or more. Just make sure you write daily.

CHAPTER 11

The Defining Moments of a Beginner Freelance Writer

Just as it happens to everyone. Beginner freelance writers do suffer major setbacks. Sometimes, days, weeks and months pass by and you can't figure out what you have achieved. You want to go back to the drawing board, but that isn't an option. You examine the steps you have taken, and confident you have been doing it the right way (Yet, you haven't achieved your goals). You ask yourself some questions again:

- What's freelance writing really?
- Are people earning through freelance writing?
- If people do, what is wrong with my approach?

The Defining Moments

There are defining moments for a beginner freelance writer. These moments will determine how far you will go in the industry. They will separate those who understand freelance writing and those who don't. These are the moments you should watch out for in your career, because they can make or mar you.

In this chapter, I will examine the five major defining moments of a beginner freelance writer, what it means and how you should approach them.

When to Start

One of the major moments of every beginner freelance writer is when to start. Many times, it is difficult to figure this out as everything looks so good. You wonder how it is possible for someone to write for others, and get paid for that.

You imagine, how easy the steps highlighted for every beginner freelance writer will materialise. You don't know if you should leave your full-time job to begin the career as a freelance writer, or you should start part time. You continue in that cycle for a while.

What you Should do

As a beginner, I will advise you to take actions immediately. Actions separate doers from dreamers. If you have read about freelance writing, and eager to delve into it, you should start doing it now because tomorrow could be too late

How to start

You have read a lot about the different ways people earn through freelance writing.

The Options: Content Mills, Freelance Job Websites or the Pitching Method

How they work

- **Content mills:** As the name implies, these are websites where different categories of contents are written on, and paid for. What a content mill does is to allow you to write on different aspects, upload it and sell.

    While it is easy to sell on content mills, you do so at ridiculously low prices. Content mills have made writers worthless, as anybody can go there, write and get paid. The result in the long run, is that you work more and earn less.

- **Freelance Job Websites:** These are the bidding sites, where buyers and sellers meet. Here, as a freelance writer, you register for the services you can offer. Likewise, buyers come to request for them.

Writers bid for available jobs on the website, and clients test and pick a freelance writer whom they are satisfied with his service/ price.

Bidding websites pay higher than content mills (but some writers have misused it too). The competition is stiff and the interests of writers are rarely protected by the websites.

- **The pitching method:** This is another way to make a living as a beginner freelance writer. It allows you to be in charge of the day-to-day activities of your job. Here, it's your duty to look for clients, pitch them on the services you offer, and charge them too on the acceptable price you want. In fact, you are the boss. This could be a bit confusing for beginners who could ask:

- How do I find clients?
- How/ what should I write to them?
- How will I get the clients' contacts and so on

What you should do

Having examined the major ways in which freelance writing can take.

What's the best way?

As a beginner Freelance writer, I will advise you to be wary of content mills (it could tempt though), but it's bad for your career. Freelance bidding websites are good for you as a beginner, but it shouldn't be your goal. You can gather the necessary experience through this. Make some cash and get clients there too, but don't stay so long here (It could affect your career in the long run).

The pitching method to me, is the best way to go. It seems difficult but as it is said: "uneasy lies the head that wears the crown".

Where to specialise

After identifying when and how to start, the next big step is to specialise. In freelance writing, your area of specialisation is your niche, which I discussed in the last chapter. What do you consider before choosing a niche?

- Are you passionate about it?
- Do you have the knowledge of it?
- Are you experienced in it?
- Is it relevant to your potential clients?
- Is it profitable?

Discussing the above listed points:

- **Passion:** This is an unnegotiable factor in choosing a niche to specialise in as a beginner freelance writer. You must be passionate about your niche and be ready to write about it anytime, any day and anywhere. A niche which you are passionate about will be easy to research on and write about. When you have more clients and more work to do, the passion keeps you going.

- **Knowledge:** This is an important consideration for choosing a niche. Your knowledge about that niche must be thorough. You should be able to write about it with minimal or no research. Your clients will expect more from you as a professional, and an in-depth knowledge of your niche will help you a great deal.
- **Experience:** Experience will help you a lot in choosing a niche.
- Are you a retired Banker/ Financial analyst? You can take up the finance niche.
- Were you once a counsellor? You can take up the personal development niche
- Have you ever taught in a high school, or any academic institution? You can take up the education niche.

With the requisite experience, you are expected to know a lot about the niche.

When clients see you are experienced, they will trust and want to work with you more.

- **Relevance:** In choosing a niche, you should be sure that it's relevant. As a rule, you should know that what is relevant in a particular market isn't the same with the other. Take for instance, topics of interest to the US market, won't be the same for the UK market. Therefore, you must study your market, and identify the relevance of your niche there before settling for one.
- **Profitability:** You are in freelance writing to make money. It is only when you make money that you can foot your bills, and take care of your family. You should search for profitable niches that enable you to get well paying clients.

What you should do

Before choosing a niche, you must examine all the points raised, as any mistake made here could be detrimental to your career.

A Blog, a Writer Website or What?

As a freelance writer who chooses the pitching method as explained above. A blog or a writer website is important to you. So what's it all about, and how will it aid your career?

- **Blog:** A blog is an online platform where a writer expresses his opinion and provides solutions to problems in his niche. As a freelance writer, a blog is an avenue to show your expertise and establish authority too.

How relevant is a blog to a freelance writer?

1. It provides a platform for you to speak to the world
2. It helps to sharpen your writing skills
3. It gives you the opportunity to show and sell your products
4. It aids in establishing yourself as a Professional. And lots more.

- **Writer Website:** A writer website is your online office as a freelance writer. It is through this website you can get in touch with clients all over the world. Display your portfolio, testimonials, the clients you have worked with and so on. You can also embed a contact/ billing form where clients can get in touch with your various projects. Clients get to know more about you through this website.

As a beginner freelance writer which of them do you need?

A freelance writer needs both a blog and a writer website. This is because with a blog, you can showcase your expertise to the world, and people will recognize you. And with a writer website, you are making your business more professional.

Taking winsomewriter.com as an example, it's both a Blog and a writer website. Writersincharge.com is both a blog and a writer website too. Though, you can have a different blog and writer website, like Carol Tice who operates her blog at makealivingwriting.com, and a separate writer website.

What you should do

As a beginner freelance writer, these two platforms are important to your career. Make a wise choice today by leveraging them.

Getting your first client:

This is the moment that defines your freelance writing career. Experts in freelance writing have opined that getting the first client is the most challenging and difficult task for a freelance writer.

This is because, as a beginner, the industry is still strange to you, and the clients will be sceptical about working with you. But as soon as you get the first client, then you can welcome yourself into the industry.

What the first client does for you

- It gives you the motivation that you are on the right track
- It gives you a reassurance that your efforts have not been in vain

- It gives you the opportunity to earn your first few dollars from writing
- It provides an opportunity for you to show the clients, your writing prowess.

So, what should you expect from your first client?

- **More work:** You should expect your first client to offer you more projects to work on, if he is satisfied with your writing
- **Earning:** At first, the pay might not be as high as you wanted, but you shouldn't settle for less because you are desperate
- **Testimonial:** Having done the first project for your first client, you can request a testimonial from him/ her. With a testimonial, you can include this on your website as a proof of projects you have executed in the past.

What you should do

As a beginner freelance writer, getting your first client is the most defining moment of your career. It can make or mar you. Your first client heralds you into the world of freelance writing. So prepare well for this day and put in your best to make sure that you deliver a quality project on time when it comes.

On a Final note

Every career has its defining moments. A beginner freelance writer, should be watchful of all these moments. If you can handle them well, and take the necessary steps, it would go a long way to determine what you would achieve. If you joke with them, it will make you detest freelance writing forever. It is never too late to take the bold step today.

Question

As a beginner freelance writer, what has been your defining moments?

Are you satisfied with your actions and inactions during these moments?

Activity

Have you chosen a niche yet? If no, do so with the tips highlighted in this chapter

About the Author

AbdulGaniy Shehu is a Writer, Online Entrepreneur, Content Marketer, and the Chief Content Strategist (CCS) of Winsome Writer Services (http://winsomewriter.com). He is a contributor for The Huffington Post, Entrepreneur Middle East, Engadget, Tweak Your Biz, Tech Cocktail, and a host of other online platforms.

He graduated Magna Cum Laude from the University of Ilorin with a degree in Mathematics.

As an Undergraduate, he participated in over a dozen writing contests, winning a handful in the process.

During his stay in the University, he was an active participant in Campus Journalism, and reported for media outlets in Nigeria such as The Cable, The Nation and Daily Trust Newspapers, among others. He's a Freelance Writer, Ghost Writer, Blogger and Content Marketer for hire.

- He helps businesses achieve their marketing goals, by writing quality web content and leads for their marketing campaigns
- He helps businesses create content such as Blog Posts, E-books, Case Studies, White Papers, and Newsletters tailored to meet their needs, take off the content creation pressure from them, hence helping them get more sales and generate more leads
- He helps businesses create automated marketing tools, simplifying difficult terms, and giving them the needed leverage to capture more leads.
- He specializes in creating unique online content for small business owners and entrepreneurs, which portray their brand with the visibility they deserve, and keeps their readers and customers coming back for more.

Whatever your writing needs are, you'll always find him as a perfect match.

Get in touch, and let him create valuable content that impact your online brand.

Conclusion

Freelancing has finally come to stay. It's now an acceptable profession that has contributed tremendously to the economies of countries. Freelance writing on the other hand, plays a critical role in the gig economy.

With this book, I'm sure your knowledge of freelance writing and what it entails has greatly improved. Becoming a freelance writer isn't a day's job, but this book highlights the major steps you need to become one in no distant time. What differentiates those who finally do, and those who don't are the actions you take. I can assure you that if you begin taking actions today, your dream of becoming a freelance writer will be fulfilled.

The steps highlighted in the book are straightforward, to ensure that anyone who doesn't have a grasp of freelance writing in the past, can become one within a month or less. It's through these steps that I became a full time B2B freelance writer, even though English isn't my first language.

If you are willing to follow these steps, you can move up the ladder from being another wannabe freelance writer to someone who earns consistently through it.

I believe nothing can stop you from achieving your dream; go take actions and take up your position as the go-to freelance writer the world has been waiting for.

I wish you all the best!

Connect with Me

Thank you for buying and reading my books. Remember to leave reviews, and also get in touch with me through my blog, and other social media platforms.

☐ Blog: http://winsomewriter.com
☐ Email: shehu@winsomewriter.com
☐ Social Media Platforms:
☐ Facebook
☐ Twitter
☐ LinkedIn

www.ingramcontent.com/pod-product-compliance
Lightning Source LLC
Chambersburg PA
CBHW020439220526
45464CB00002B/777